A New Life and other poems of Living Passion

Trisha Georgiou

Also by Trisha Georgiou

My Name Is A

Quartered Enlightenment

A New Life and other poems of Living Passion

Trisha Georgiou

40 pages

Published by 918*studio*

ISBN-10: 0985194456

ISBN-13: 978-0-9851944-5-1

Copyright © 2014 Trisha Georgiou

Printed in the United States of America

All rights reserved

Cover & interior design by Rivertown Creative & Co.

*To all who are Living their Passion
and for Ciaran.*

Preface

Passion, a simple word, which elicits beautiful emotions and states of being.
Passion brightens colours, purifies sounds, focuses our mind while giving purpose to our lives.
Passions create biochemical changes within our bodies and minds and spirits, propelling us to the heavens, grounding us to Earth, and connecting us to people of like mind.
Passions enrich our souls and each second of our lives.
This chapbook was created to capture and illustrate passion. It was created to help inspire, and put words to feelings we share while we discover and embrace our Living Passions.

With prayers and candles burning,

Trisha Georgiou

Contents

Realignment 1
A New Life 2
Living Passion 4
Celtic Love Spoon 6
Bookmaker 8
The Playwright 9
Seven Decades 10
The Conductor 12
On Broadway 14
Preservation Hall 15
Inauguration 16
Pulse of the Cities 17
Art Talks 18
Perennial Wisdom 20
Faith Healing 22
White Smoke 23
Living Passion 24
Mother's Love 26
Acknowledgments 29

Realignment

Stones played like chess pieces
placed perfectly in house.
Gazing down the sheet, I see
five stones of two colours
with one opposing on the button.

So far they are winning,
but we have one stone left.
This end falls on me,
the anchor, the skip.

Never before have I felt this weight
not just from the stone.
My first time delivering
the hammer in show.

I have thrown a thousand times
even more in my mind,
with breath, nerves, thoughts,
and passions in sync.

My foot on the hack
the rock in balance, steady
I quiet my mind, inhale
then release.

With perfect force
the sweepers guide.
The stone sails past the hogline,
to knock them out of line.

A New Life

We hiked across
the rugged shoreline,
gazing west
over the ocean.

I look to find
a life once lived,
those memories
faded in this beauty.

Our stroll continues
through this new town.
A rest taken,
an outdoor cafe.

A cuppa tea,
a piece of cheese,
a shortbread biscuit,
of Irish making.

The stroll continues
through fields of green
with flowers blooming
of every colour.

Hand in hand
we lay in the clover,
staring at the heavens
who blessed, us meeting.
For it is here
in this new land
which, I thought
I'd never be.

Divine words, stories
being written,
passions discovered
a new sense of me.

Living Passion
for Liam Ryan

Time ticked down, the game tied.
Overtime escalates emotion.
Adrenaline rushes, bounding pulses,
yet, muscles in exhaustion.

On the field, earth beneath
my knee, I knelt in subconscious prayer
remembering, living every game.
An eternity passed in seconds.

Victories celebrated.
Losses endured.
All push through the goal
for great achieving.

Coaches, team mates
engrained in my soul,
spirit and memories
eternally within me.

The dew and sweat beneath my knee,
the play began as planned.
I received the ball, but
now, kicked from my hands.

The fate of this game
is in destiny's hands.
The ball is kicked in the air.
We wait, seconds, then cheers.

Today, victory shined her eyes upon us
as the ball drove between the goals.
Month, years, of hard work, I spent.
The Shamrock Bowl is ours.

The Vikings hold the trophy
but the win, for me is much deeper.
Every practice, game, win, and loss
guided my life and passion.

Celtic Love Spoon

Rings, wrinkles matching
years of life, growth
evidence of storms weathered.
One this limb, the swing hung.
His grandfather pushed him
now, he is the grandfather.

In his workshop holding, embracing
connecting with the memories, the history,
held within the branch of this tree
which lived generations before he.

Slowly, he debarks this branch
exposing the soul within.
What new life is in store?
What is meant to be created
from this piece of wood
with generations of memories?

He sits at his workbench in prayer
unifying spirits of three.
Running his hands over the grain,
he touches the memories,
connecting to the art
handed down to him.

Tools, knives sharpened in a row
each one has a purpose.
He lets his inner knowing guide.
Gentle strokes, a scraping sound
like angels singing, fills the quiet space.
Curls of wood fall like autumn leaves
on to the floor of the workshop, a sacred space.

Shavings fill the air with scents of his grandfather.
Childhood memories are pulled
from the recesses of his mind.
Hours pass, entranced
in his passion,
forming, carving each twist
of an endless Celtic knot.
A shamrock adorns the top
symbolizing his heritage, his blood.
The spoon's bowl is then rounded out
a welcome communion.

Bookmaker

Typesetting, fonts,
places letters
forming words,
turning into sentences,
turning into pages,
bound together for purpose.

Words, crafted from life,
a writer living their story.
Breathing words.
Bleeding emotion,
onto page after
page of history.

This is what I do.
My passion, my love
of words, books, life
binding these pages
forming the spine
of the writer's dream.

The Playwright
for Shea Doyle

Friends and strangers gather
uniting to become one audience.
They (I) filled with anticipation
yearning to experience,
moving art, live performance.

A nervous excitement abounds backstage
costumes, makeup, my soul.
Every detail accounted
a new life of characters I created.

The men and women in black
never seen or heard
vital in totality
sets and props move magically,
lights on and off
essential ambiance for my creation.

Where did this all begin?
In my heart, my life, my soul
stirring my mind
then penned to paper, dialogue captured,
elicit change, thought, lessons, laughs,
the living passion of the playwright.

Seven Decades
for Keith Clayphan

On the garden path beneath my feet,
I stand grounded, living
this moment, this breath
for I have walked for seven decades.

My journey, this brick path
was not always smooth
free from weeds and moss
but, it was always sturdy.

I turn around to look at my past steps,
Am I proud of the path I made?
For each brick is a memory
cemented in mortar in my mind.

Though I see each brick,
where have these seventy years gone?
Some bricks were easier to place
yet, everyone fit perfectly.

John Deere & Co. gave me many,
my blood still runs green.
Between those bricks were others
just as sturdy, sealed together by love.

Bricks with etched names of
Son, Brother, Husband, Father, Grandfather, and Godfather
repeated throughout my journey
and carried forward onto the new bricks I place.

Now I look ahead,
What is my path? What bricks will I lay?
Bricks with cricket, woodworking, gardening will be formed.
What else?

The Conductor
for Zack Morton

Music, sounds, drumline beating.
Marching my spirit
down the path of my passions,
awakening senses of my authentic life.

The reeds; nimble counterpart,
quickening thoughts,
fill my mind
with flowing melodies.

But, it is the brass that rings.
Singing to my soul,
connecting my heart, my mind,
harmonizing my being.

This room where I stand, teach,
filled with these instruments and acceptance.
It is a place of safe expression
for the creative force within me and them.

My students gather from different genres
their paths joined
to make one sound
learning to move together in formation.

One hundred twenty-four souls
look to me for rhythm and direction.
I was chosen only a few weeks ago
to guide them at home and on fields away.

I do not just count steps and notes,
but guide breath, growth, and life.
This is my purpose, realized long ago
in a band room where I was the student.

Now, I hold the baton at first season's end.
The circle from dream to reality complete.
Surrounded by friends, love
 A shooting star said,
"This is only the beginning."

On Broadway

Stage lights
costumes music
billboard names
stars tonight.
Thousands more
want dream
to see
their name
neon lights.
Hours years
practice rehearsals
sing dance.
Bones muscles
tired numb
push forward
through pain
gain advantage
reach perfection.
Curtain call
curtain rises
backstage nerves
instantly gone
music plays
actors escape
lose themselves
living performing
their passion.

Preservation Hall

Established 1961
The Jaffe's began the legacy
where jazz is still
playing today.

Along the French Quarter
the legend remains
untouched, unchanged
the essence, the music, sings.

Mixed bands, integrated sounds
Color was blind and embraced
opened doors for people
passionate, with grace.

Preservation Hall Jazz Band
traveled the world enlightening
natives to the sounds
of New Orleans.

Timeless, classic
standards in music,
now, son Ben swings,
opening eyes and minds.

This rich culture, New Orleans jazz
we cannot afford to lose.
Preservation Hall, Thank you
for being a living museum.

Inauguration

Fingers brush over bound spines
from works of great poets,
her mentors,
aligned side by side.

One by one, each held, adored
wishing to afford, each copy
without the means,
but passion, galore.

Her fingers find, a single poem.
Richard Blanco's One Today.
She dumps her purse to find loose change.
The Presidential Poet, she will be.

Pulse of the Cities

Motion driven by purpose.
Buses, cars, trucks racing to destinations
on the veins of the Cities.

Beat, rhythm, sounds, voices,
dynamics driving progress forward
is the heart of the Cities.

The pulse is the passion of the people.
Children creating perpetual motion,
advancing life in the Cities.

We are making noise.
We are finding our voice.
We are creating art in the Cities.

We are composing our symphony.
We are dancing our ballet.
We are changing the world.

Art Talks
for Bruce de Gouveia Carter

Week upon week, now
adding up to decades,
I have conversations
between artists.

One thousand and counting
artists of all genres
living, doing, breathing,
their passions, their art.

How has our interview, our encounter,
influenced, changed, enriched, led
the life of the artist, me,
the listener?

People allow me
into their lives,
homes, cars, minds
and even spirits.

Some I know, many I won't.
It doesn't make it less important
or less life changing
to not know every receiver.

Yet, the connection and opportunity
for growth is there, waiting
for me to ask the right question
to spark and feed the flame of passion.

Half way up the hill in a sound booth,
on Augustana campus
I have met artists living their passion
while I live mine.

Exploring the mind and creativity of our guests
gaining advice to
steer the young artist.

Perennial Wisdom

Hours spent, tea in hand,
half way up a flight of eight.
Sometimes watching, mostly thinking,
longing for words and poems to make.

Surrounded by pots of seasonal friends
and those dear herbs who move
from indoors to out.
They whisper ideas and rhymes about;

Rosemary, she remembers everything
and protects the garden's gate.
Lavender brings peace and calm
to all my mental states.

Daisy faces look to toward the Son
a smile they always bring.
Roses of all colours
each have their own song to sing.

Basil, Thyme, and Oregano
all share their terracotta home.
Their scents from Heaven, touch my kitchen
provide a healing touch, I am never alone.

Mint, my aggressive friend.
He grows and grows and grows.
His purpose are many
in the stories told.

Sage, my master teacher,
the oldest of them all,
Wisdom from ancient teachings
brings special gifts, when I call.

Weeping Cherry stands tall
at the bottom of the stairs.
He cascades ideas and spring flowers
grows fruit to eat and share.

My purple friend, oh Butterfly Bush
you climb inspiration up the railing,
providing a feast for hummingbirds
and butterflies, angels inviting.

Half way up, a flight of eight
I am surrounded by love and friends.
Who bring to me peace and joy
the essence I need to create.

Faith Healing

On my knees
bowed down
beneath the cross,
I place pain
on the altar.
My passion,
my gift,
my curse,
I collect pain,
taking it from others.
Pain resides in the body
from the mind and spirit.
With my healer's touch,
I take their pain
into my hands.
I place it
where pain was bared first
on the altar
with candles burning.

White Smoke

The world awaits
the white smoke
puffing from the roof top
symbolizing a new dawn.
I see.

People in all walks from most lands
pray for **Me** to come,
listen to their desperate prayers
their pain, their brokenness.
I hear.

Pain from illness,
pain from fear,
pain from destruction,
pain from -,
pain from loss of passion and hope,
I feel.

In their soul they know **Me**
even when hope is lost.
Prayers for peace come deep within
the heart of the soul
where joy reigns.
I touch.

This white smoke will restore hope,
peace to the common man,
faith back in **Me**,
hatred banished.
I know.

Living Passion
for Ciaran O'Sullivan

Time ticked down, the game tied.
Overtime escalates emotion.
Adrenaline rushes with bounding pulses
yet, muscles in exhaustion.

Time out, I called. They look to me,
an oasis of calm in the storm,
for I played many years, I wore their shoes.
I understand what goes on.

Coaching isn't to dictate plays
or grab the winning spotlight.
My coaching, my passion
is to teach, mentor, and guide,
so they can lead and play their game.

Plays were run. Now, a good field position.
a chance for a field goal to be made.
Another timeout called by the opposing team
to throw our iced kicker off key.

He stood shivering on the field from more than the cold,
but our team's heart beats as one.
They huddled together giving more than warmth
but strength for the last second of battle.

The whistles blown, the team is set.
The ball thrown back to Liam.
Danny kicked, drilled it in
between the posts, for the WIN.

Victory shined her eyes upon us.
Months, years, hard work, prevailed.
The Shamrock Bowl title is ours.
The Vikings won the trophy.

For me, victory is just the polish on the cup.
My Living Passion is the game
and guiding the team is truly
what's in my blood and soul and mind.

Mother's Love
for Elsa, Zane, & Finley

Our eyes met, the first time,
but I already knew you.
I heard your heartbeat
as you did mine.
I felt you grow, stretch,
As you grew, I grew for you
in my body and mind.

Life changed instantly.
Life became worth living.
Suddenly, my life has purpose
passion and meaning.

Acknowledgments

While writing this book I received many life-changing gifts from inspiring individuals. Thank you for letting me share and capture your life and passions. Robin Throne, 918*studio,* thank you for making books while giving endless opportunities for writers. Thank you for sharing and understanding the writing passion. Thank you for your vision and expertise.
Keith Clayphan, thank you for years of love and support. Happy Birthday. Bruce Carter, WVIK, Augustana Public Radio, Thank you for your artistic gifts and promoting arts in the Quad Cities. Zack Morton, Director of Bands, Moline High School, May you always push the bar of excellence skyward. Coach Ciaran O'Sullivan and Liam Ryan, thank you for coaching me to experience the thrill of winning Shamrock Bowl XXIII. Sandra Marchetti and Jodie Toohey, your friendship and review of this collection are appreciated. Shea Doyle, thank you for years of creative support, inspiring works, and reviewing this collection. Thank you to the Bettendorf Public Library for your support of poetry and local poets. "Pulse of the Cities" was a finalist in the Library's Poetry in Motion contest. To Dewey's Copper Café, Moline, Illinois: thank you for keeping the coffee brewing.

Finally, to my writing family at the Midwest Writing Center: your mission for the written word is forever appreciated.

Helvetica Neue

Helvetica was originally developed in Switzerland in 1957 by Max Miedinger with Eduard Hoffmann. It was initially called Neue Haas Grotesk.

Neue Helvetica is a reworking of the typeface with a more structurally unified set of heights and widths. Other changes include improved legibility, heavier punctuation marks, and increased spacing in the numbers.

Helvetica is widely known by both designers and laypersons alike for its legibility and its proliferation in our everyday world. For example, the New York Subway System uses Helvetica on its signs.